ANDREW CONQUERS THE COURT

Inspired by a True Story

written by **Antonietta Tripodi Quinn**

illustrated by **Eva Morales**

Written by Antonietta Tripodi Quinn
Illustrated by Eva Morales

Photograph of Antonietta Tripodi Quinn by Kathy Pieters Photography

Photograph of Eva Morales (self-photo)

Photograph of Andrew in 12th grade holding the ball: Lisa Gresens Photography, lgresens@gmail.com, www.lisagresens.smugmug.com

Photograph of Andrew dunking in Ronald McDonald Game: Christopher Cecere Photography, rochesterccphotos@gmail.com, www.rochesterccphotography.com

Published by Miriam Laundry Publishing Company
miriamlaundry.com

Webster, New York
Library of Congress Control Number: 2023918744

HC ISBN 978-1-77944-015-0
PB ISBN 978-1-77944-014-3
e-Book ISBN 978-1-77944-013-6

FIRST EDITION

This book is dedicated to my husband, David, and my two sons, Andrew and Sean.

Your encouragement and support made this book possible. I'm the luckiest wife and mom in the world!

A special thank you to Coach Fenton, Coach Cray, and all the coaches who have played an integral part in Andrew's development as a basketball player. Also, to Wil and Jackson, I am so grateful for the boys you are and the friendship you have with Andrew.

Today was the day! Andrew jumped out of bed and got ready for school.

Today, Andrew was trying out for the school's fifth-grade basketball team. He had played basketball for as long as he could remember, and he loved the game!

4

At the end of the school day, Andrew rushed to his locker to put on his sneakers. He couldn't wait to get on the court!

Walking to the school gym, one of his friends called to him. "Hi, Andrew! Are you ready for tryouts?" asked Will.

"I am so ready!" Andrew replied. "How about you?"

"Can't wait," Will answered.

In the gym, Andrew grabbed a ball and started to warm up.

Tryouts started. "Let's see how fast you can run!" Coach shouted.

All the boys sprinted up and down the court.

Next, the coach divided the boys into groups. Each group took turns shooting foul shots, three-point shots, and lay-up shots. Andrew was sure Coach would be impressed with how he shot the ball.

Lastly, the boys formed two teams. "I want to see how you play defense," Coach explained.

The teams played a game against each other. Andrew just knew he did a great job!

At the end of tryouts, Coach said, "Come by my office after school tomorrow. I'll let you know if you made the team."

At the end of the school day, Andrew walked quickly to the coach's office. Coach handed him an envelope.

Andrew rushed out of school. His dad was in the parking lot, ready to pick him up. He jumped into his dad's car and ripped open the envelope.

Thank you for trying out for the school basketball team.

I am sorry to let you know that you did not make the team.

I hope you will continue to work hard and try out again next year.

Coach

ANDREW

"What does it say?"
asked his dad.

"I didn't make it,"
Andrew mumbled.

Andrew's dad sighed. "I'm sorry, Son. I know how much you wanted this."

Andrew slumped in his seat.

"You could try out again next year," his dad suggested. "You can keep practicing."

"I guess," Andrew answered.

Andrew's mom was waiting for him when he got
home. He looked at her with tears in his eyes and
shook his head.

"I'm so sorry, Andrew," said his mom. "Did the
coach tell you why you didn't make the team?"

Andrew showed her the letter. After reading it, she asked, "Do you think you should ask Coach what you can work on for next year?"

Andrew shrugged. "I guess so," he said.

The next day at school, Andrew saw his friends in the hallway. They were all talking about the upcoming basketball season.

Soon, Andrew realized he was the only one in his friend group who didn't make the team! *But why?* Andrew wondered.

Andrew remembered his mom's advice, and after school, he went to the coach's office.

"Coach," said Andrew. "Do you have time to talk?"

"Sure," Coach replied. "What's up?"

"I wanted to ask why I didn't make the team." Andrew swallowed. "What could I have done better?"

"It was a hard decision for me," Coach answered. "But there are some skills you can work on to become a stronger player."

"Like what?"
Andrew asked.

"I'd like to see you play better defense," Coach said. He smiled. "Once you learn how to do that, you'll be unstoppable."

"Better defense," Andrew murmured. "Okay. I ... I can do that."

"I want you to work on *all* your skills. Promise me you'll be back for tryouts next year."

"OK, Coach. Thanks for the talk."

15

After school, Andrew started shooting baskets in his driveway. His friends came over and asked if he wanted to play a game.

"Yes!" Andrew replied. He wanted to show them that he should have made the team.

But as they played, he missed every shot, lost the ball while dribbling, and the players he guarded scored every time. He played terribly!

Maybe I wasn't good enough to be on the team, Andrew thought.

Andrew went upstairs to his room. Lying on his bed, he wondered if he should give up playing basketball. As he lay there, he saw the quote from one of his favorite basketball players, Dwayne Wade, on the desk in his room.

Andrew read that sentence over and over.
I have to believe in myself! He decided
then and there that he was going to
become a great basketball player.

Andrew started playing basketball any time he could.

He got up early each morning to practice his dribbling skills.

He joined his town's travel basketball team.

In the spring, he joined a second travel team with older players and learned from their experience.

His friend, Jackson, had a basketball court in his backyard. In the summer, Andrew rode his bike to Jackson's house every day to play with him.

21

When he could not find anyone his age to play with, Andrew played in the driveway with his younger brother, Sean.

Sean's job was to rebound the ball so Andrew could keep shooting.

Fall, winter, spring, and summer,

Andrew practiced, practiced, practiced.

Finally, the basketball season tryouts arrived.
Andrew felt confident.

He could run faster, shoot the ball better, and his defense was stronger than ever. *Would Coach notice?*

The next day, Andrew went to Coach's office after tryouts.

When Coach handed him his envelope, he looked at Andrew and smiled. Andrew ran to his dad's car and tore open the envelope.

After a week of playing together, the coach chose his starting line-up for the first game. Andrew couldn't believe it when Coach called out his name!

The season was a success! The team went undefeated, and Andrew was the team's leading scorer.

At the awards celebration, Coach called
Andrew up to the podium. "Congratulations!
You are our MVP of the year!"

Andrew was stunned — *Most Valuable Player*.
He thought about the days and weeks and
months of practice, and he smiled.

Andrew in 8th grade

Andrew in 12th grade

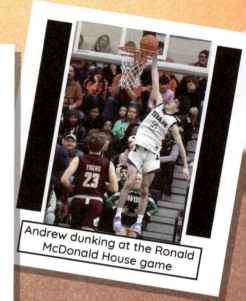

Andrew dunking at the Ronald McDonald House game

This book was inspired by a true story. Andrew is the author's son. He didn't make his school's seventh-grade basketball team, and he was devastated. Andrew will now say that it was a defining moment for him. He decided to work harder than ever to make the team the following year. Andrew made the school team in eighth grade and was a starting player!

Andrew never looked back. He continued to work on his skills, and, as a freshman at Webster Thomas High School in Webster, New York, he 'played up' on the junior varsity (JV) team. His first year on JV was a learning experience for him, but in 10th grade, he became a starting player. Andrew also started on the varsity team in 11th and 12th grade. During his senior year, other teams and coaches noticed Andrew's talents. He was voted the Monroe County Division 2 Co-Player of the Year, a Ronald McDonald House All-Star Player, and the MVP of his high school varsity team. He was also voted onto the First Team of the All-Greater Rochester Basketball Team. He has been an inspiration to others, including his family.

At the time of this writing, Andrew is studying architecture and playing college basketball at Marywood University in Scranton, Pennsylvania.

Printed in the USA
CPSIA information can be obtained
at www.ICGtesting.com
LVHW061250211123
764112LV00014B/658